Step-by-Step Investing

A Beginner's Guide to the Best Investments in Stocks

Joseph Hogue

About this Book

Wall Street has brainwashed both of us!

It's brainwashed you into thinking that you need to 'beat' the market to achieve your financial goals. Is it a coincidence that to do this, you need to pay for advice and brokerage fees from those same Wall Street firms?

Wall Street has also brainwashed investment analysts like me. We're made to believe that everyone needs our advice and that advice needs to be a complicated strategy of timing and trading.

It was only when I got off Wall Street and onto main street that I realized the truth. **Spend enough time with real investors and you realize they just want a simple investing strategy that will help reach their financial goals.** They want it laid out in a way that's easy to follow and they don't want to lose sleep every night worrying about their money.

That's what this book is about!

This book is the first in a series of four, outlining a step-by-step process for a simple investing strategy. This book will get you started in what investing is really about and how to build an investing plan that's right for YOUR goals.

We'll start with the ten basics of investing that every investor must know and how to actually win the stock market game. I'll show you how to get started investing and a step-by-step approach to build your own investing plan.

In this book you'll learn:

- The only way to win the stock market game by playing it YOUR way (pg. 11)

- The 10 basic rules of investing that will keep you from making the bad investment decisions that cost people money (pg. 15)

- How to pick investments that are right for YOUR goals (pg. 54)

- How to maintain your portfolio without having to watch the markets every day, or even every month (pg. 61)

Check out the other three books in the Step-by-Step Investing series to round out your investing strategy. You'll get everything you need to lay out a sleep-at-night investing strategy that will meet your financial goals.

I've put nearly a decade of work as an investment analyst into the series and hope you can use it to develop a simple strategy that will meet your goals. If you find the ideas useful, *__please leave a review on Amazon__* to let others know.

Joseph Hogue, CFA

Born and raised in Iowa, Joseph Hogue graduated from Iowa State University after serving in the Marine Corps. He worked in corporate finance and real estate before starting a career in investment analysis. Mr. Hogue has appeared on Bloomberg as an expert in emerging market investing and has led a team of equity analysts for sell-side research. His investment analysis has been featured in advisor newsletters, institutional research reports and in the financial press.

He holds the Chartered Financial Analyst (CFA) designation, the gold standard for ethical and professional conduct in investment management.

PeerFinance101.com is a new kind of personal finance blog where readers share their own stories of personal finance challenges and success. There's no one-size-fits-all solution to meeting your financial goals but you'll find a lot of similarities in others' stories and a lot of ideas that will help you get through your own challenges.

Click through to PeerFinance101 for topics from investing to managing debt as well as retirement planning and frugal living.

Step-by-Step Investing: A Beginner's Guide to the Best Investments in Stocks

ISBN-13 (eBook) 978-0-9962321-4-2
ISBN-13 (Print) 978-0-9962321-5-9

Contents

How to Start Investing and Why it Can't Wait!

I understand that it's not always easy to put money aside after all your bills are paid. I've been there, living paycheck to paycheck. It's easy to talk about investing and saving when you've got extra cash. It's not as easy when you're trying to support a family and worrying about the essentials.

But that makes it even more important to get started now. Even if you're only able to save $50 a month, you can build a great nest egg if you start early enough.

It's called compound interest but is really just a fancy term for making money off your money. Start investing in your 20s and you'll be earning interest on that money for decades as well as earning interest off your interest. The graphic below shows the power of investing early and growth in $50 monthly contributions starting from different ages.

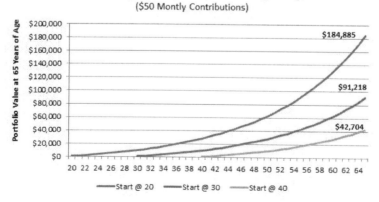

Investing: The Benefit of Starting Early
($50 Montly Contributions)

Invest more than $50 a month and you'll see even bigger benefits to investing early.

But the best reason to start investing is to change your role in life. Living paycheck to paycheck means you're always renting from the owners of wealth. Investing in stocks, bonds, real estate and other assets means you are an owner rather than a debtor. You own the assets that other people rent and can control your own financial future.

It's one of the keys to financial freedom, stop renting your life and start owning it!

How to Start Investing for your Financial Freedom

The first half of the book will be dedicated to laying the groundwork for your investing plan. We'll cover how to prepare your budget and how to avoid the biggest investing myths that cost people money.

In the second half of the book, we'll work through a simple investing strategy from how to open an online account to making sure you have the right stocks for your financial goals.

I've spent my career analyzing stocks and learning how to manage people's investments. The simple truth though is that you really don't need all the technical insight to do very well. In fact, sometimes all the investing strategies cause more problems than they're worth.

That's why I wrote this book and the other three in the series, to share a simple investing strategy that will work for you and your needs as an investor.

It's only through being an owner of assets that you'll be able to achieve the financial freedom that many take for granted. I know it can be intimidating to start investing and planning for your future. You don't have to jump at it with everything you've got but it's so important to just get started.

Don't Start Investing until You Read This

How many times have you started putting money away for investments, only to withdraw it after a few months? Even if you have managed to keep adding to your investments, how sure are you that you'll meet your financial goals?

Too many people fail to lay the groundwork before they invest their money, only to see their portfolio crumble and their hard-earned dollars disappear.

I use the road trip analogy a lot with investing because it leads to one of the most important but neglected concepts. You wouldn't just get in your car and start driving without knowing where you were going. Why do so many people start investing without knowing their financial destination?

Despite all the time spent talking about what stocks to buy, only a small part of investing is picking the actual investments. It's much more important to understand your long-term goals and the best strategy to get you there. Lay the right groundwork with planning and the right investments will fall into place.

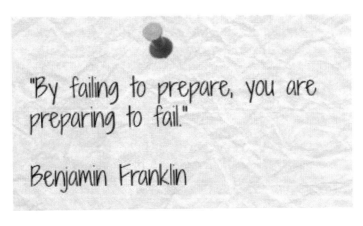

"By failing to prepare, you are preparing to fail."

Benjamin Franklin

Invest? With What?

Almost everyone agrees with the need to save for their financial goals, but who has the money? Even with low unemployment, the economy never really jumped higher after the financial crisis and wages have only grown at the rate of inflation. It's all you can do to pay the bills and hopefully have enough to treat the family to a night out every once in a while. Besides, you've got social security for retirement, right?

Even if the rules on social security aren't changed, and they almost certainly will have to in order to cover the massive future shortfall, the average check is just $1,230 a month. That may cover a roof over your head and something to eat but you'll be hard pressed if you actually want to enjoy your retirement.

You don't have to put hundreds toward investing every month. We've already seen how just $50 a month can grow to hundreds of thousands. Don't think you can even save that much? Try turning your budget upside down!

Most people start their budget by listing out income and then subtracting expenses. When they finally get to savings, there's nothing left.

Try a different approach to budgeting.

- Start you budget by taking out how much you want to invest each month. The general rule is 10% of your income but you might want to start with a little less to make sure you can meet the goal.

- Then list your expenses out. If there isn't enough money to cover all your expenses, cut from those instead of cutting your savings amount.

- If you've got a little extra after expenses, put some of it to saving and have fun with the rest. Life is about living, not about skimping and sacrificing until your 85 years old.

It's best to start small. Start with a regular contribution of what you know you can afford and then increase it if you can. I have seen too many people jump into investing and expect to put half their paycheck in an account. When bills come due, they end up selling their investments and never really enjoy the benefit of making money from their money.

The best investing you can do is before you begin investing

The question I get asked the most is, "What is the number #1 reason investors lose money?" The answer is easy, because they start investing without a plan.

Without a plan, they don't know how much money they need to meet their goals. They don't know how much risk is involved and how they'll react to losses. As a result, they stumble through years of investing without ever really getting anywhere.

Preparing an investment plan will help you establish key points:

- What are my financial goals?

- How much do I need and how much do I need to invest?

- How much risk am I comfortable taking in my investments?

- What about emergency cash and debt?

Establishing your financial goals is an obvious one but gets overlooked by most investors. What do you want to do with the money? Without something to look forward to, many investors lose the motivation to invest and end up withdrawing money.

Besides putting a dollar amount on your financial goals, which we'll get to, really sit back and think about what life will be like when you get to your financial destination. Build an image around your goal by thinking about where you'll live and what you'll do for fun. This kind of visual exercise is going to help drive you during those times when money gets tight.

For the amount you'll need to meet your financial goals, start with the big expenses like retirement, education and buying a home. Get a good idea of how much you'll need for the big stuff before adding on the smaller goals.

If you plan on changing your lifestyle during retirement, you'll need to plan out how much it will cost. Otherwise, the standard rule is that you'll need between 65% and 80% of your current income in retirement.

Retirement calculators on the internet can be confusing but you don't need to be exact. You only need an estimate for how much you'll need and what kind of annual return you need given the amount you can invest on a yearly basis.

Most people are surprised at the modest return they need when they actually plan out their financial future. To meet my own financial goals, I only need a return of about 4.5% over the next few decades. Had I not known this, I might be tempted to put too much money in risky stocks to try for returns of 8% or more. Why take all the risks with your financial goals if it's not necessary?

Once you know the annual return you need to meet your financial goals, it's time to look at the level of risk you're comfortable with taking in investments.

Most investors just throw money at stocks, not understanding that there are other investments that are less risky and that can provide a stable source of return. Investors end up freaking out when stocks take a tumble and panic-sell at exactly the wrong moment. Understanding your risk tolerance is about avoiding circumstances that will cause you to lose sleep and make bad decisions.

There are risk tolerance questionnaires on the internet, but finding your comfort with risk is pretty easy.

1) How many years do you have until you need to depend on the money?

If you have more than ten years to invest, you'll have more time to take advantage of higher returns in stocks without worrying about a stock market selloff. If you have less than ten years, you can't afford to take a big hit because you might not have time to recover.

2) When you see the stock market and your investments fall rapidly, does it cause you to lose sleep?

If you're uncomfortable with big changes in wealth, you will want to put more money in safer investments.

3) What kind of investments do you usually prefer?

Do you go for the high-flying, risky investments or do you generally prefer the slow-and-steady approach? There's nothing wrong with taking a little more risk if that's what you like but understand your comfort level before you invest.

4) How stable is your income?

You can take a little more investment risk if your income is more certain. Tenured professors have an almost guaranteed income so they can take more investment risk. People that work in the financial sector might take less investment risk because their income can rise or fall quickly depending on the economy.

Knowing your risk tolerance will help decide how much of your money to put in stocks, bonds, real estate and other investments. I've put together a chart of risk in different investments.

The Risk – Return Tradeoff

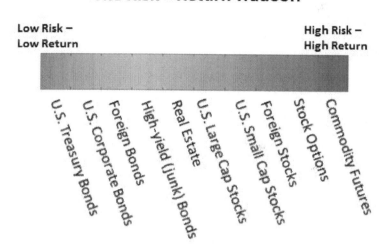

We'll get to how to decide the amount of money you put in each later in the step-by-step portion of the book.

You'll never meet your goals if you constantly withdraw money from investments. Besides money for everyday expenses, it's also smart to keep some aside for emergencies. Most people try keeping at least three months' worth of expenses in a savings account to pay for life's little roadblocks.

If this seems impossible, start with a month's worth of expenses and add to it a little each month. The important point is to not touch your investment account.

What to do with debt is also a question I get frequently. You should try to reduce the amount you owe on credit cards and other debt but **I have seen too many people put off investing forever because they never get their debt down to where they want it.**

A good rule is to pay off debt with interest rates above 10% and make payments on other debt while you begin your investing plan. This will help ensure that you use your money wisely now and still meet your long-term goals.

Action Steps:

- Put a rough dollar amount on how much you'll need in retirement.

- Figure out how much you can comfortably save each month and use a retirement calculator to find the annual return you need to meet your retirement goal.

- Understand your risk tolerance. If you need a high annual return to meet your goals but have a low risk tolerance, reevaluate how much you can save or how much you need to retire.

- Pay off high-interest debt but don't put off investing to be debt-free.

How to Win the Stock Market Game

Winning the stock market game is a matter of knowing which game you're playing.

It's no secret that investors are notorious for underperforming the stock market, realizing returns far below the general market. Data for the ten years through 2013 shows that the average investor earned an annual return of just 2.6% compared to a return of 7.4% for stocks and 4.6% for bonds.

10-Year Annualized Investor Returns (2004 - 2013)

Source: Dalbar, Bloomberg

In hindsight, we know why we lose. Investors chase high-flying stocks they hear about on TV only to realize they must have been the last to jump on the bandwagon as the price comes crashing down. Panic sets in and the investor sells out of the stock just before it levels off or stages a rebound.

So why is it so hard to win the stock market game? Why can't investors conquer their bad habits and earn a better return on their investments?

The answer is because most investors are playing the wrong game!

Let's look at the game of tennis. Tennis is truly a game of contrast, you are either really good or really horrible, and your skill level determines your strategy for winning the game.

Two professionals playing the game will need to do everything they can to score points. They each know that the other will make few mistakes so the key to victory will be in taking risky shots for the ace.

By comparison, when my wife and I play tennis, the strategy is very different. I can try for the risky shots and get lucky on a few but, more often than not, the ball is going to go soaring over the fence and I'll be running after it. Since it's more fun to return the ball back as hard as possible, practicing my best guttural grunt as if I were John McEnroe, I make a lot of these errors and my wife usually wins.

She knows the key to winning this amateurs' game is to just concentrate on getting the ball back over the net...**and making the fewest mistakes.**

It turns out, winning the stock market game is a lot like winning in tennis.

The Professionals' Stock Market Game

Professional money managers are measured against the rest of the managers in their investing style. Around the beginning of the year, you'll see rankings come out placing managers among the 'median' return for their group.

Since everyone is constantly trying to score a few extra percentage points to put them above the median, the professionals' stock market game is about taking risks to beat everyone else.

It turns out that even the professionals have a tough time playing their own game. Data from 2012 mutual fund performance shows that just 39% of professional fund managers beat their index while the average fund return actually trailed the stock market (S&P 500) by a percent after fees.

If the **average** fund return was only 15%, there's a good chance that a lot of 'professionals' lagged the rest of the market by a wide margin.

Why? Because they are making big bets and losing big when those bets don't pay off. They're trying to serve an ace but hitting the ball into the bleachers!

Do Professionals 'Beat' the Market?
Mutual Fund Returns versus the S&P 500

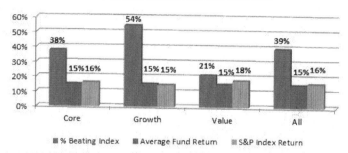

■ % Beating Index   ■ Average Fund Return   ■ S&P Index Return

Source: Lipper Analytical Services, BofA Merril Lynch (2013)

The Amateurs' Stock Market Game

By comparison, most of us won't face losing our job if our investment returns fall short of the 'average' investor. We only need to avoid making the big mistakes and meet our long-term financial goals.

Just as my wife doesn't have to play like Steffi Graf to beat me at tennis, you don't have to invest like a pro to win the stock market game.

The amateur game is played by understanding the basics and sticking with a simple approach. Don't get caught up in trying to find stocks that will double or trying to beat the market. Stick with the basics listed in the next chapter and avoid making the big mistakes.

The beauty of the stock market game is that you can pick your match. You're free to play the professionals' game, analyzing stocks daily for the slimmest of chances at a few extra percentage points. You're also free to play the amateurs' game, investing for the long-term win on making fewer mistakes.

It's your decision; just make sure you know which game you're playing.

Action steps:

- Understand that investing isn't about huge returns that 'beat' the market. Keep to the basics and a simple plan that will meet your needs without a lot of mistakes.

The Top 10 Investing Basics

We've got two more chapters before we start on the step-by-step investing strategy you can use to meet your goals.

We'll cover the top ten basics of investing in this chapter. Whether you've been investing for three years or three decades, remembering these basics will help you avoid the big mistakes that cost people money.

It can be intimidating for new investors to get started because there is so much information out there about investing. People scream at you from the TV and the amount of internet 'analysis' available is enough to make most people put it off entirely.

The good news is that getting started is pretty easy if you just follow the basics. In fact, unless you're working in finance and managing other people's money, the basics are all you'll ever need to meet your financial goals.

Investing Basics #1: Understand what Investing is All About

The most important thing to remember about investing is to understand what investing actually is…and what it is not.

Investing is not gambling and it is not about picking winning stocks that will make you rich. Yeah, sorry about that but it's a truth that the industry doesn't want you to know.

You see, keeping the public thinking that investing is about making huge returns means you're glued to the TV or internet for every piece of information they churn out. That's worth billions in advertising for the TV stations and websites.

Investing is about making money on your money, over a very long time. It's about owning something that will be worth more in the future.

As a stock owner, you actually own a piece of the company in which you invest. Understanding which stocks to buy is really about two questions:

- Do I really want to be an OWNER of that company? Is it a company that will be around forever or is it just a fad?
- Does the investment sound like a 'bet' that the stock will jump or is it based on the idea that the company has solid long-term potential?

Investing Basics #2: TV Pundits and Analysts are NOT there to make you Money

There is good investment advice to be found on TV and online but the vast majority of it is there for one purpose… to be entertaining.

Why? Because viewers and readers are worth advertising dollars. That in itself is not a bad thing, providing investment ideas so that people will visit your blog or channel. The problem is the extreme to which many blogs and TV stations have taken it. The line between investing and entertainment has blurred so much that it's difficult to see the difference anymore.

One successful money manager on TV has been reduced to screaming, leaning on buttons that make all kinds of noises, and throwing things at the camera just to keep his audience entertained.

That's not investing; it's an annoying morning radio show.

It's a happy coincidence if you make money on this kind of investing advice but the goal is to be entertaining and persuasive.

It's ok to check out some ideas in the financial press and on investing websites but before you click that 'buy' button on your investment account:

- Does this investment fit with YOUR personal investment plan and tolerance for risk?

- Have you looked at the long-term potential for the stock or are you solely going off the advice of the analyst?

Investing Basics #3: Investing is all about YOU

One of the biggest things missing from stock recommendations is one of the most important in investing…you!

Your investment plan is about your goals and the risk you'll need to take to earn a return on your money. The problem with following investment advice is that it doesn't take into account if the advice fits with your plan.

Within your personal investment plan, you're going to look at how much you need to meet your financial goals and what kind of risk you are able to take. Not making a personal investment plan is like going on a road trip without knowing the destination or how to get there.

Once you have an investment plan based on your needs, it becomes pretty easy to sort through all the stock advice because it's clearer whether the investment is right for you. You'll trade in and out of stocks less frequently and save a ton of money in fees.

Investing Basics #4: Diversification isn't just something you Think about in Investing

Diversification is your number one tool in meeting your investment goals. It's one of the most talked about ideas in investing but few investors actually do it correctly.

Investment diversification is about owning a wide range of asset classes (stocks, bonds, real estate) and different investments within each asset class. Stocks, bonds and real estate all offer different benefits and react differently to economic factors.

The idea of investment diversification is that, if stocks were to take a tumble, your bond investments would be there to smooth out your total portfolio return. If energy prices dropped, taking stocks of energy companies lower, then your stocks of consumer goods companies might do better.

Everyone talks about diversification but greed keeps most people almost entirely invested in stocks. The average investor holds just 15% of their portfolio in bonds. The fact that older investors hold a much larger percentage in bonds leads me to believe that younger and new investors hold next to nothing in safer fixed income investments.

We'll talk about how to make sure your investments are diversified in the step-by-step section of the book.

Investing Basics #5: If you can't beat them, join them

Investors and the financial press talk so much about 'beating' the market that new investors take the goal as a given. Everyone is trying to earn returns above that of the general market...and few are actually able to do so.

The first problem here is that investing isn't even about 'beating' the market. It's about earning the return you need to meet your financial goals, whether that return is above or below the market return.

The second problem is that constantly trying to beat the market has most investors trading in and out of stocks, paying huge fees and losing money over the long-run.

Don't even worry about how much the market went up or down in any given year. It doesn't matter. Invest according to your own need for return and for your financial goals.

Investing Basics #6: How Many is Too Many?

One of the problems with constantly watching the financial media is that an investor can pick up ten great stock 'ideas' every day. They end up spending hours analyzing each and a portfolio of hundreds of individual stocks.

You really don't need that many stocks to diversify your portfolio and you'll see the fees add up with every purchase. Research by Dresdner Kleinwort found that the risk in a portfolio matched the market risk after about 30 stocks.

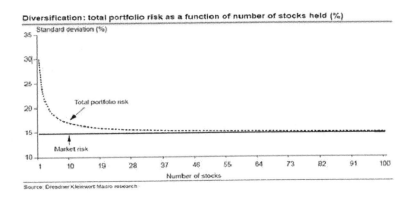

That means you've lowered your risk down to the general riskiness of the entire market after just 30 investments.

What does this mean to your strategy? Holding a large portion in a few exchange traded funds (ETFs) will give you exposure to hundreds of companies and all the diversification you need. Use the rest of your money for stocks, say around 25% of your stock portfolio, to invest in ten individual companies. Limiting yourself to ten individual stocks will mean picking only those with the most potential over the long-run.

Investing Basics #7:Don't Supersize your Portfolio

Nearly all brokers or stock investing websites will offer accounts on margin. Margin is just borrowing money to invest more than your portfolio value. If you have $100 in the account, you might be able to buy three times that in stocks.

Investors are tempted by the upside potential on margin investing. A 5% return on your $100 means an extra $5 at the end of the year. That same 5% return on your $100 plus $200 in borrowed money means an extra $15 at the end of the period.

Don't do it! Just don't!

Investing on margin works the other way as well. That relatively minor 5% loss when the market hits a weak patch becomes a much bigger loss when you're using margin. When the stock market lost 50% of its value over the 17 months to March 2009, someone trading on margin would have quickly lost everything.

Those borrowed funds aren't free either. Stock trading sites will charge upwards of 8% or more a year in interest fees, eating away at any gains you make during good times and amplifying your losses during bad times.

I interviewed one reader recently that lost more than $30,000 by investing on margin. Robert got caught in the massive selloff in coal stocks starting in 2014. He started off with just 5% of his portfolio in Peabody Energy, the largest U.S. coal producer, but kept investing more money as the price plummeted.

Even after he was fully invested, he was able to keep plowing money into the stock by borrowing on margin. By July 2015, the shares had tumbled 92% and he was on the hook for huge losses plus the interest on his borrowed money.

Resist the temptation to buy on borrowed money. It's gambling and that's not what investing is about.

Investing Basics #8: Go West young man...Way West!

We've already hit on the idea of diversification but even the most diversified stock investors still fall short in one category, investing in international companies.

While the United States used to be the engine of global economic growth, today the U.S. accounts for just a fifth of the global economy. This fact seems to be lost on investors that have an average of 85% of their investments in companies based here in the red, white and blue.

Sure, U.S. companies get about a third of their sales from customers in other countries so you are getting some international diversification by investing in large American firms. The fact is, there are other reasons to invest in international companies and you need more diversification than that provided by foreign sales to U.S. companies.

- Business cycles don't match up from country to country so buying foreign company stocks means you benefit from growth in one economy when others might be slowing

- Stocks of foreign companies are not as popular with investors so prices are not usually not as expensive as those of U.S. companies

Investing Basics #9: Easy does it

Too many new investors get excited about investing and put every spare penny into the account. They end up putting more in investments than they can afford and need to withdraw money to pay for other expenses.

This sets up the idea that it's easy and ok to regularly sell investments and withdraw money, an idea that will cost you big time over the long-run.

Just as bad, new investors get excited about the idea of making lots of money on their investments and hover over the computer screen watching daily fluctuations. The euphoria of seeing a percent or two gain in one day leads to depression when stocks decline on another day.

All this just distracts the new investor from their long-term investing goals. A lot of new investors end up getting discouraged or burn out on investing, withdrawing all their money and closing the account.

- Deposit only as much in your investing account as you can have locked away for a very long time. A good place to start is between 5% and 10% of your overall budget but your own needs will dictate how much you save.

- Understand that investing is about long-term (greater than five years) goals and that weekly, monthly or even yearly results may not mean much. Watching your investments on a daily or weekly basis is way more stress than you need.

Investing Basics #10: Investing is about what you put in

Returns are great and can add up over a lifetime of investing, but investing is just as much about what you put in.

To be truly successful and reach your financial goals, you need a plan for regular deposits into your investment account. Putting money in every once in a while or just when stocks are going up isn't going to cut it.

That's because a big portion of your overall portfolio is going to be the deposits you make.

In fact, on regular deposits and a 7% annual return, it's not until the 20th year that your earnings amount to more than your deposits. Even after 30 years, deposits account for nearly a third of the overall portfolio value.

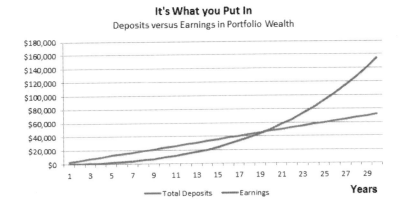

It's What you Put In
Deposits versus Earnings in Portfolio Wealth

Investing is a lot better than a savings account but it is still about regularly putting more money to work. Build regular deposits into your budget and watch your wealth grow steadily over decades.

Investing isn't really that complicated and these ten investing basics are likely all you'll ever need to meet your financial goals. Focus on these ten and don't make investing more complicated than it needs to be.

Action steps:

- Read through each investing rule and think about how it applies to your plan and your needs.

- After reading through the book and working out your investing strategy, revisit the ten investing basics to make sure you are following them.

- Check in on the basics every year or so to make sure you haven't strayed from these simple rules.

Mutual Funds and Exchange Traded Funds: Opening the Markets to Everyone

This is the last chapter before we begin our step-by-step plan but a very important one that will help you meet your goals with as little risk possible.

Mutual Funds and Exchange Traded Funds (ETFs) are basically the same investing option with a few important differences. Mutual Funds were created to offer regular investors access to the kind of expertise and diversification that only the rich enjoyed in the early days of investing. Exchange Traded Funds came around much later to lower fees and provide the advantage of stock-like trading.

Mutual Funds: A History of American Dreams

Mutual funds are just a collection of investments packaged together and managed for the investor's convenience. For this convenience, investors pay a fee every year to the fund's managers. Funds have been around for centuries but really came to market in the 1950's and exploded in popularity over the last several decades.

Before mutual funds, access to the stock market was limited to those with huge fortunes. Advisors and brokers were not as numerous or normally willing to take on clients without sizeable fortunes. The vast majority of the population was doomed to park their savings in bank accounts and had little hope for wealth creation.

Mutual funds changed all this and there are now thousands of options for the investing public. With a mutual fund investment, investors can get professional management and a basket of stocks for instant diversification.

More than 7,000 Funds, which one is right for me?

The sheer number of mutual funds available can make it impossible to choose the right one. Even if your employer only offers a smaller group of funds for your retirement plan, the choice can still be tough.

Fees are one of the most important things to watch for in fund selection. Annual management fees normally range from 0.2% to 2% and are calculated as a percentage of your total investment. That means you'll pay out $2,000 in fees every year on a $100,000 investment.

Some funds may also include fees that you pay with each contribution or when you sell the investment. Obviously, lower is better for fees and you should always compare fees across a few funds within the same investment category.

The real risk to fund selection is that many advisors have hidden motives behind the advice they offer. Some fund companies pay advisors for guiding investors to their funds so you may only be shown those funds that pay the highest kickback to the advisor. If you decide to let an advisor help you select a fund, always talk to a couple of different advisors to get the complete picture.

If you decide to select your own funds, look for the investment styles that meet your needs. Index funds generally just invest in a broad category and carry the lowest fees. There are also funds that invest in specific sectors, company sizes, along with a myriad of investment rules. A newer option is funds that target a specific date in the future and are designed to match the investor's portfolio with the time they have to retirement.

ETF Investing: The New Kid on the Block

Exchange-traded Funds have been available since 1993 in the United States and were created to address many of the problems with mutual funds. ETFs basically run off of the same idea as mutual funds, a collection of investments packaged as one product, but trade like any other stock in the market.

Because ETFs trade like stocks throughout the day on the market, you get an immediate price when you buy or sell. This isn't the case for mutual funds which only trade at the market close. You put in an order for a mutual fund and the price could change dramatically before that order is filled at the end of the day.

ETFs are also generally less expensive than mutual funds. You will pay a transaction fee to buy or sell, just as you would any other stock but these are usually much lower than the percentage fees you pay to buy or sell a mutual fund. ETFs also charge an annual management fee but it is usually much lower than mutual funds, around 0.15% to 1% per year.

Taxes can be a huge drag for mutual fund investors. Because of the way the funds are set up, the constant buying and selling within the fund creates a taxable event for investors. That means you could be paying taxes on the fund's gain every year whether you sold any of the investment yourself. With ETFs you only have to pay taxes when you personally sell the investment.

Do I still need mutual funds?

Because ETFs are generally traded like stocks and are not as actively sold to investors, they often do not come with the same level of advice and assistance as mutual funds. For this reason, some investors still seek the advice of advisors and buy into mutual funds. They may end up paying more in fees and taxes but can rely more heavily on advice from an expert.

I am a big proponent in ETF investing and use the funds to round out my own portfolio. A few diversified funds can really lower the risk in a portfolio of individual stocks poised for growth. Look for funds with lower expense ratios and that provide the diversification you need against other investments.

A few of my favorite ETFs:

SPDR S&P 500 (SPY) – This fund is the largest ETF and holds all the stocks in the S&P 500, the largest companies in America.

Vanguard Emerging Markets (VWO) – This fund holds more than 1,000 stocks of companies based in fast-growing countries across the world. The stocks are a little more volatile than the huge American firms but have a better chance at growing over the long-term.

Vanguard REIT ETF (VNQ) – This fund invests in real estate investment trusts, companies that buy and manage real estate. We talk more about REITs as a great income investment in the Step-by-Step Dividend Investing book. The fund is a great way to get exposure to real estate investments without the hassle of managing property yourself.

Vanguard Dividend Appreciation ETF (VIG) – This fund invests in stocks with a record of increasing their dividends. Companies that return money to shareholders and regularly increase their dividend are a great way to build your portfolio over time.

All of these funds charge super-low annual fees less than 0.2% and will give you exposure to thousands of stocks. With most of your money in stocks invested in a few funds like these, you can put the rest in a few individual companies without having to worry about constantly picking stocks.

Action Steps:

- Consider investing in a few ETFs that cover broad market themes like the entire market, emerging market stocks or real estate investments. These funds will give you an investment in hundreds of stocks for one commission and will reduce the risk in your portfolio.

- After you are done putting your investing strategy together, look for a few ETFs that fit with your risk tolerance and need for return.

A Step-by-Step Investing Strategy

This chapter begins our step-by-step process for building an investment plan that fits your needs. We'll cover the mechanics of opening an online investing account and buying stocks first as well as some of the pitfalls to avoid in online investing.

In the next chapter, we'll cover investing ideas and how to decide what to put in your investing portfolio. In the final chapter, we'll cover the steps in how to maintain your investments and how to know when to sell your stocks.

The theme of the book and the entire step-by-step series has been to create a simple plan that will meet your goals. That won't change in the next few chapters and you should always keep the basics of investing in mind when developing your plan.

Should you Buy Stocks Online or through an Advisor?

In most regulated markets, only certified professionals can buy stocks. These stockbrokers pay for a seat on the exchanges and make their money from fees or commissions when people give them orders to buy or sell. If you've got a lot of money to invest, you might talk directly with a broker but most individual investors work with an advisor or an online platform which itself deals with the broker.

Advisors make their money through a few different options. They may charge a commission every time you buy or sell.

They may also make money through kickbacks when you buy a certain mutual fund. These two methods have fallen out of favor because it leads to a conflict of interest. The advisor wants you to buy and sell as often as possible or to buy certain funds even if they are not necessarily right for your needs.

The financial advisor industry has lately been switching to a fee-only method where you pay a percentage of your total wealth each year. This helps to remove one conflict but may cause another. Unless you've got a nice size nest egg, the potential fee might not be enough for the advisor to give you the time of day.

Even if a fee-only advisor agrees to take you as a client, that management fee can add up. The 1% difference on a $200k account can mean a difference of $374,000 over 30 years compared to an account with no fee. The advisor may also be tempted to trade in and out of stocks to try for the big win and justify their advice. Why would anyone pay for an advisor that just buys and holds stocks?

Online investing websites have become the solution for most investors, offering the ability to buy stocks online without an advisor. These websites like TDAmeritrade and E*Trade also offer some advisor services but the concept is a DIY investing tool so you can save on fees.

I've been buying stocks online since I got out of the Marine Corps in 2001 and have several accounts on different sites. It may seem unnecessary to have more than one online investing account but different sites offer different features. Most online investing sites charge no annual fees so there's really no cost to having more than one account.

Step 1: How to Open an Online Investing Account

Opening an online investing account is nearly identical on any of the websites. You'll first be asked basic personal information like name, address and to choose a username/password.

Then you will fill out a list of questions on your income, wealth, investing experience and occupation. Much of this is to classify you around your experience with investments and risk.

The online investing sites have a duty to only offer investing options that are suitable for an investor's level of experience. Someone with no knowledge of options trading and margin should not be given access to these without helping them understand the risks first. It turns out that you probably don't want access to these kinds of investments anyway. They just complicate your investing strategy and can add a lot of risk to your portfolio.

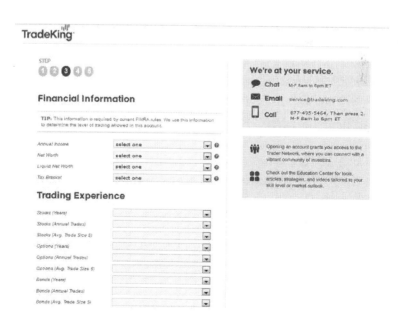

You will answer questions about your occupation and whether you are considered an 'insider' at a company as well. These are set by regulators so the online investing site can monitor trading by people that might have non-public information and could break the law by trying to profit from it.

I've included a comparison list of online investing sites at the end of this chapter. It doesn't include every site out there but all the most popular websites with the best options for fees and ease of use.

After your account is reviewed and approved, and there are very few reasons why it wouldn't be approved, you will link it up to your bank account with the ABA and routing number. This will allow you to transfer funds more quickly and easily than a snail-mail check. The minimum with which you can open an online investing account varies but is generally $500 to $1,000 for non-retirement accounts.

Some websites will allow you to set up automatic withdrawals from your checking account each month to deposit into your investing account. I'm undecided on this feature. It's a great way to make sure you invest regularly but can lead to fees if you don't have money in the account when the withdrawal goes through. Either way, just make sure regular deposits are a part of your investing plan.

Once inside an online investing account, the features and options can be overwhelming. Most online investing sites offer excellent customer service and will guide you through some of their tutorials on the phone. It never hurts to call up customer service after you open an account and ask them to show you the most used features and how to get around the site.

All online investing sites will offer general information on each stock traded in the market as well as some basic analysis. Many will also offer 3rd-party research analysis from companies like Credit Suisse and Morningstar. As an investment analyst, this is my main reason for having multiple accounts to be able to review research reports from different companies. You probably won't need the majority of features offered on an online investing site and sometimes the most basic sites are the best.

Again, it's all about making investing as uncomplicated as possible. Our step-by-step approach will basically be just finding a good mix of investments that's right for your needs and then holding them for decades. You won't need the daily analysis and features offered on most investing platforms.

Since we are not focusing on a particular online investing site, I decided to use Yahoo Finance as an example of the basic information you'll see for a stock. This is a pretty common layout and there are a few points on the graphic below that you should understand. You won't necessarily need all the points when you go to buy a stock but it makes it less intimidating to know what some of the information means.

1) The name of the company, price per share of stock and the change in price will be listed at the top.

2) The Bid price is how much someone is offering for the stock while the Ask price is the price at which someone is offering to sell their stock. For most stocks, these prices will be really close and you won't need to worry about it. If the stock or fund does not have much volume (see below) the bid and ask price may be farther apart. If this is the case, it will affect how you buy the stock online which we will highlight below.

3) The beta is the general riskiness of the stock compared to the overall market. A stock that generally moves up or down closely with the market will have a beta close to one. Stocks that are much more risky than the market will have a higher beta while less risky stocks will have a beta of less than one. Most people don't look at the beta but it can be a good guide to understand the potential risk in an investment you're considering.

4) The 52-week range is the highest and lowest price at which the stock has traded over the last year. While it won't tell you if something is really expensive or cheap, I always just like to notice if the stock is trading at its high-point or near the low. I'm frugal to the core and always think twice about buying something that is around its most expensive point. By the same

token, there may be a good reason that a stock price has plunged to its low and you will want to know why before you buy shares.

5) Volume is the amount of shares that are trading so far that day and the average amount of shares traded each day over the last three months. If there aren't many people buying and selling the stock, then the bid and ask price may be farther apart. You might have to pay a little extra to buy the shares or take a price discount to sell the shares if the average daily volume is less than a few hundred thousand shares. It won't be an issue for the largest companies but will be something to consider if you are going to buy stock in smaller companies.

If the day's volume is significantly higher than the average, there might have been some news released about the company. You will want to check this out to make sure it doesn't affect your decision to buy or sell the stock.

6) Market capitalization is the total worth of shares issued by the company, a rough measure of the size of the company. One way to classify companies is by their size:

- *Nano-cap companies* (below $50 million) and micro-cap companies (up to $300 million) are extremely small and risky investments. They are generally penny stocks and may not have to provide all the financial information required by regulators. Risk of total loss is very high and these companies are generally not suitable for individual investors.

- *Small-cap companies* from $300 million to $1 billion in market cap are still fairly risky but can provide some upside growth to your investments if you diversify enough.

- *Mid-cap companies* from $1 billion to $5 billion still offer some of the growth potential of smaller companies but the stability of larger firms.

- *Large-cap companies* ($5 billion to $200 billion) and mega-cap companies (above $200 billion) are the giants of the stock market. They might not grow as quickly but offer more stability in their size.

7) P/E or price-to-earnings ratio is the stock price divided by how much in net income per share the company has booked over the last year. It's the most popular measure of value used by the market but may not really mean anything.

The P/E ratio is a relative measure, meaning it only tells you how cheap or expensive a stock is compared to its own history or to other stocks. It doesn't really tell you if the investment itself is a good buy. If a stock has a P/E of 15 against another stock with a P/E of 20 – there is nothing to say that both are expensive or maybe both are cheap. We only know that one is *relatively* cheaper than the other. Similarly, the potential for earnings growth may be much better for the second stock and justify the higher valuation.

It is also very easy for management to manipulate earnings on a financial statement. All kinds of expenses like depreciation and the cost of inventory can be made to look higher or lower, making earnings rise or fall artificially.

I include P/E here as one of the points you should know on a stock only because it is so popular and you'd think it odd if I didn't include it. The fact is that the measure really doesn't help you in investing and you shouldn't let it affect your long-term investment strategy.

8) The dividend and yield are an important point for many investors. Stocks that pay dividends usually pay them out in four installments throughout the year, regularly increasing the payout if the company can afford it. The yield is the percentage of the dividend divided by the stock price, a return you will get just from the regular cash payments.

I'm a big fan of dividend-paying stocks and love getting paid for just holding an investment. Income stocks are one of the best forms of passive income and are highlighted in my book, The Passive Income Myth.

Step 2: How to Buy Stocks Online

The process of buying stocks online is nearly identical across different online investing sites as well. I've pasted an image of a trade screen below.

1) The tabs at the top allow you to buy different types of investments like stocks, options, mutual funds and bonds. Most people will only ever need to buy stocks and bonds. Mutual funds have been replaced (in my opinion) by lower cost exchange traded funds (ETFs) which are bought just like stocks.

2) Your order type will be to buy or sell the investment

3) Quantity is the number of shares you want to buy or sell. Divide the total amount you want to invest in the stock by the price. You should never hold more than 5% of your total stock portfolio in a single company. Hold too much in one stock and you risk big losses if something happens to the company. Diversify across many stocks or funds and you won't have to worry too much about any one particular company.

4) Your price type will usually be 'market' and will buy the shares at the best available price between the bid and ask prices.

For stocks with very low volume where the bid and ask price are more than a few pennies apart, you might consider placing a 'limit' order. Placing a limit order means you put in a price at which you are willing to buy or sell the shares. It's a way to control the price you pay for the stock but the commission you pay may be a little higher. For the majority of stocks, the bid and ask price will be so close that the higher commission paid on a limit order will not be worth saving a penny or less on the price.

5) Once you preview your buy or sell order and click through the next screen, your order will go active. For most stocks on most online investing sites, your order will be processed in less than a minute.

Investing Risks to Avoid with Online Investing Sites

Online investing sites will offer you a ton of information on investments from research to technical charts and strategies. The process for buying and selling stocks online is so easy that you will be tempted to 'trade' your investments, jumping in and out over very short periods trying to make a quick profit.

Resist this temptation at all costs. The online investing sites make their money on commissions so they want you to buy and sell as often as possible. It's hidden in the idea of you making more money but it will end up costing you much more in fees and taxes.

- With all the people on TV screaming to buy, buy, buy and the online investing sites providing more information than you can use it is just too easy to trade in and out of stocks. The average investor makes 17 trades a year according to statistics on TDAmeritrade investors. Even on the most inexpensive online investing sites, that amounts to nearly $100 a year lost to commissions.

- Investing on margin seems like a great idea until you're sitting with your head in your hands wondering where the money went. Online investing sites will allow you to borrow money against your account (margin) and buy more stocks than you could afford otherwise. If your stocks start falling, you stand to lose a lot of money and could easily see your entire account wiped out. Don't invest on margin…ever.

Some Online Investing Sites to Consider

I have accounts with four online investing sites and set my wife up with an account on a fifth site to take advantage of different research and features on each. Most investors will not need so many accounts but don't overlook the advantage of having more than one account. Some sites may offer a lower cost while others may have a particular feature you like.

Investing Site	Cost Per Trade	Minimum Account	Features
E*Trade	$9.99	$500	Online Banking, No-fee Funds, Dividend Reinvestment
Scottrade	$7	$2,500	Online Banking, No-fee Funds, Dividend Reinvestment
TDAmeritrade	$9.99	$0	Online Banking, No-fee Funds, Dividend Reinvestment
Capital One Investing	$6.95	$0	Online Banking, Dividend Reinvestment
Motif Investing	$9.95	$0	Motifs
TradeKing	$4.95	$0	Dividend Reinvestment
Merrill Edge	$6.95	$0	Online Banking, No-fee Funds, Dividend Reinvestment

A lot of the sites have moved into online banking, offering bill pay and debit cards on your account. I haven't used this option on any of my accounts but it does make managing your finances even easier to have everything in one place.

Most sites also offer a list of ETFs or mutual funds that you can buy without a commission. This is a huge advantage, especially if you are going to be buying more of the fund regularly as you deposit money in the account.

The best return you'll ever make on your investments is the free money you get through retirement tax savings and commission-free investments. Don't pass up the opportunity when it comes along.

I've included Motif Investing to the list for its innovative way to buy stocks. The site doesn't offer a lot of the features found on other online investing websites but you can buy a group of 30 stocks for one commission. You basically are making your own ETF except you don't pay an annual management fee. It makes for a very cost-effective way to invest in individual stocks and you might want to consider it for the non-ETF portion of your portfolio.

While you will pay the basic fee to buy or sell stocks, you'll want to watch for a few other fees that might be on each site.

- While you may be able to open an account with no minimum, some sites may charge an annual fee for accounts with less than a certain amount.

- Some sites may charge a fee if you do not make a minimum number of trades over a year. This isn't usually a problem if you regularly add to your account and use the money to invest every six months or annually.

- While basic customer service questions will be free, you will have to pay a fee to have someone help you buy or sell stock over the phone. If you're in doubt how to do it, ask for basic help from customer service but then make the trade on your own through the internet.

- Almost all sites will charge a fee if you bounce a check or if a withdrawal from your checking account comes back as insufficient funds.

Action steps:

- Check out a few of the online investing sites in the table to decide which is right for your strategy. Consider opening more than one account for access to different features.

- Always make sure you understand the risks with online investing and avoid unnecessary fees.

Step by Step Investing: Two Key Concepts

This chapter will start you on two core concepts and how to actually start picking investments that will meet your goals. It may seem an oversimplification that your entire investing plan should come down to two concepts but it really can be that easy.

- *Diversification* – Investing in different assets (stocks, bonds, real estate) and different investments in each asset to make sure your portfolio doesn't all plunge with a stock market crash.

- *Life stage investing* – Investing according to how much time you have left to major purchases and the amount of risk you can manage.

Step 3: Making Sure your Investments are Diversified

We've talked briefly about the concept of diversification a few times in the book but I wanted to devote a section to the idea and how to use it in your plan.

Diversification gets a lot of talk by investors but few people really do it correctly. To understand diversification, understand that different assets react differently to the economy and other headlines. Strong economic growth is great for stocks because it usually means corporate profits are heading higher.

If you were investing in bonds, a booming economy might not be so great because it might mean higher interest rates and lower bond prices. Conversely, when the economy falls apart, stocks sink while bonds hold up much better.

If you invested only in stocks, you may have had some extremely tough times over the last 15 years. Two stock market crashes could have wiped you out completely if you panicked and sold at the wrong time. By the same token, investing only in the safety of bonds makes it difficult to meet your goals on low annual returns.

Investing in stocks and bonds, as well as other assets like real estate, means some investments rise as others fall. Your annual returns are smoothed out and you don't have to worry about your long-term goals.

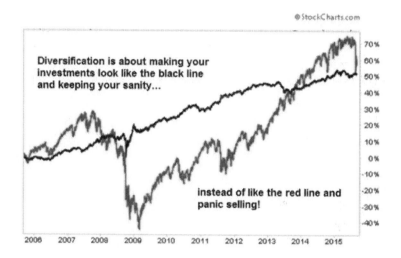

But diversification doesn't stop at just stocks and bonds. You need to hold other asset classes like real estate.

I've included tables here of the major asset classes along with the relative advantages and weaknesses in each.

Asset Class	Sub-Class	Benefits	Weaknesses
Stocks		High return potential on growth and company profits. Some cash return from dividends and protection against inflation	Since stocks are ownership of future profits, there are no stock returns if there are no profits. The high return potential lends itself to periods of investor euphoria and stock market crashes.
	U.S. Stocks	Companies operate in a stable legal structure and economy. Returns are generally more stable and certain.	More limited growth due to the maturity of the economy. Sales of U.S. companies overseas rise and fall as the dollar's value rises or falls against other currencies.
	Foreign Stocks	Other countries, especially smaller emerging markets, may provide higher potential for grow as their economies catch up. International stocks also offer diversification as their economic cycle differs from that of the United States.	Greater uncertainty around foreign government and business rules. Potential for larger crashes as investors rush in and out of smaller markets.

Stocks can also be separated by the size of the company and the different sectors in which they operate. We'll cover more on this later and how to diversify your investments within each asset class.

Asset Class	Sub-Class	Benefits	Weaknesses
Bonds		Provides a stream of income as the debt is paid but no inflation protection since payments are fixed. Provides safety since bonds get paid before stockholders.	Bonds lose their value as interest rates rise since returns are fixed. Returns are lower than stocks or real estate.
	Government Debt	Ultimate safety on bonds of large, developed nations	Very low returns just above inflation. Bonds of emerging market countries at risk of default.
	Corporate Debt	Higher return than government debt and good certainty of payment on bonds of very large companies	Some risk of default, especially for smaller companies.

Corporate bonds can be separated further into investment-grade and junk bonds. Junk bonds aren't necessarily bad investments as the name implies but do carry more risk other bonds. Recently, investors have started to put money in personal loans through peer lending platforms like Lending Club as well. These bonds are directly to other people and carry higher rates of return. We won't build them into our investing strategy but you may want to consider them as a way to diversify further across bonds.

Asset Class	Sub-Class	Benefits	Weaknesses
Real Estate		Provides stable long-term returns from cash flow and appreciation as well as inflation protection	Price appreciation on residential property is limited to population growth while commercial property prices can be volatile with the business cycle
	Direct Investment	Relatively higher returns and a tax shield from depreciation	Difficult to buy enough properties to reduce risk and management can be a headache
	REITs	Returns relatively similar or higher than stocks with slightly less risk. No management needed.	Prices are more volatile than general real estate and shares rise and fall with the rest of the stock market.

REITs are a great addition to your investing plan because they offer some of the advantages of real estate investing without the constant management of directly owning property. REITs are detailed further in the Step-by-Step Dividend Investing book along with how to build in an income strategy with dividend stocks and energy MLPs.

Within stocks, there are nine sectors in which you will invest. These are broad groups that operate in common industries in the economy. Just as the value of asset classes react differently to the economy, stocks within sectors react differently as well. Companies within utilities and consumer staples do better when the economy is slowing while energy and technology companies do better when the economy is growing.

The Nine Stock Sectors

Getting your diversification in stocks means investing in each of the major sectors. Try to pick a mix of large companies and small companies.

Financials	Energy	Healthcare
Technology	Materials	Consumer Staples
Utilities	Industrials	Consumer Discretionary

The amount you invest in companies within each sector will depend on your risk tolerance but you should hold some stocks in all nine sectors. Consumer staples, utilities, healthcare and financials tend to be a little less risky because they produce items that people need whether the economy is growing or not. The other sectors tend to rise and fall more closely with the economic cycle.

Over three to five years, some sectors will do better while others might lag a little. You can do one of two things to even out your investments.

- Deposit savings into your account monthly but wait every six months to actually invest. With your regular six month investing, split your total investment unevenly so that more is invested in the sectors that have lagged. For example, if your energy stocks have done well and total $500 but your technology stocks only equal $300 then you will want to invest more in your technology stocks to even out the sector investments.

- If you'd rather split your regular investments evenly each time you buy stocks then you can wait to rebalance after several years. Every few years, sell some investments from sectors that have done really well to invest in other sectors that have lagged. Set a specific date to do this and not more often that every two or three years.

Step 4: Life Stage Planning and Asset Allocation

While diversification across asset classes is a good idea, it doesn't mean you want to invest the same amount in each. The amount you invest in stocks, bonds and real estate will change according to your needs and risk tolerance.

The concept is called life-stage investing, and is guided by the amount of time you have left to invest and circumstances around your financial life.

Stocks offer better long-term returns than bonds and real estate but are much more risky. Younger investors with several decades left to retirement can hold more in stocks and won't have to worry about a downturn in the market. Even if stocks lose their value in a recession, the investor has plenty of time to recoup those losses when stocks rebound on the next cycle of growth.

As you age, the time you'll have available to be able to a make up for losses on riskier investments decreases. Older investors will want to hold more of their portfolio in bonds and real estate. These safer investments may not grow as fast as stocks but are more stable and will help ensure your portfolio is there when you're ready to retire.

Life Stage Investing - Matching Risk with Your Needs

Stocks	70%	60%	50%	30%
Bonds	15%	15%	25%	50%
Real Estate	15%	25%	25%	20%

* Percentages are approximate and may not be appropriate for all investors

The percentages of your money you invest in each asset class will depend on your own tolerance for risk as well as your point in life-stage investing. Younger investors that do not want a lot of risk in their portfolio may opt for more bonds and real estate than other investors.

Your choice of how much you invest in each asset class will be the biggest factor in the growth of your investments. Bonds won't grow as fast as stocks but your return will be more certain. Resist the urge to pour all your money in stocks just for a higher return if your risk tolerance won't support the risks.

Based on ten-year returns to the different assets, I've put together the average return on the example portfolios in the life-stage investing graphic.

Planning your Asset Allocation and Return

	Very Low Risk	Low Risk	Average Risk	High Risk
Stocks	30%	50%	60%	70%
Bonds	50%	25%	15%	15%
Real Estate	20%	25%	25%	15%
Potential Annual Return*	5.4%	6.4%	6.8%	6.9%

* Based on prior ten years to October 2015
- not a forecast or guarantee of return

Again, it has to be noted that these returns are based on the last ten-years and not a forecast of the returns for the future. It does help to show the tradeoff in risk and return.

Your tolerance for risk should be the main guide for how much you invest in each asset. You can adjust the amount in asset classes if you need a little higher return to meet your financial goals but you should not expect to earn very high returns and still take minimal risks.

If your need for annual return is extremely high but your risk tolerance is relatively low, the best coarse of action is to either adjust your goals or work on saving more money. Reaching for higher returns by taking on more risk will only open the door to panic-selling and other bad investor behaviors.

Just as with shifting your balances in stocks, you shouldn't shift your balance across your asset classes more frequently than every few years. In fact, since life-stage investing changes according to your age, you may hold off to rebalance your asset classes every decade. Every ten years, decrease the amount invested in stocks in favor of investments in the other two asset classes.

Action Steps:

- Decide how much of your total portfolio you will invest in stocks, bonds and real estate. Base this off of your tolerance for risk and the rate of return needed to reach your financial goals.

- Within each asset class, decide how much you will devote to sub-asset classes like stock sectors and different types of bonds.

- Write down your target percentages as a part of your personal investment plan and commit to keeping the desired proportions.

Step by Step Investing: Picking your Investments

It may seem odd that a book about how to invest should spend so little time on picking actual stocks or investments but I'm trying to get a very important point across.

Investing isn't about picking stocks!

If you only remember three points from the book, I want you to remember that:

- Investing is about the big picture, about YOUR big picture. It is not about picking great investments that will make you rich. What annual return do you need to meet your financial goals and what level of risk are you comfortable taking?

- Study after study has proven that the majority of the difference in annual return comes from your decision on how much to invest in each asset class. Invest more in stocks and you'll probably earn more but you also take much more risk. Investing in bonds is much safer but will produce lower returns.

- Even investors at the extremes, very low risk-takers or very high risk-takers, should have a mix of assets. You should always hold at least some stocks, bonds and real estate. Without this diversification, your wealth is going to jump or plunge along with the market and you'll constantly worry about the result.

Step 5: Picking your Investments

Only after understanding everything we have talked about to this point should you start to think about which investments to buy.

Investing in Stocks

The stock portion of your portfolio is your best chance at one of two outcomes, make a solid annual return or lose it all and miss your financial goals.

Which would you rather?

No investment is as hyped as stocks and this is where you really need to remember the basics. Listening to the barrage of investment advice thrown at you daily, it is way too easy to trade in and out of individual stocks in an attempt to score big.

To avoid the massive fees in trading, the bad decisions and the stress that comes with stock trading you need to make your investing plan as simple as possible.

Dedicate between 60% and 80% of the money you invest in stocks to broad exchange traded funds. Investing in a few funds that cover a large portion of the market will do a few important things for your portfolio:

- ETFs give you instant diversification with hundreds of individual stocks. You won't have to worry about any particular company's results because it's only a small fraction of the investment

- ETFs help take the hype out of investing. People love to talk about individual stocks, buying and selling the hot topic of the day. ETFs don't get hyped as much by investors and are much more the buy-and-forget investments

- ETFs are much cheaper than buying individual stocks. You can buy an ETF with one commission or you can pay hundreds of dollars to buy 10 or 20 individual stocks

Keep in mind two issues when choosing your exchange traded funds. Make sure you are diversifying into different types of stocks by geography, sector and size of company. Compare the management fee for each fund. There are enough funds available that you shouldn't have to pay more than 0.5% in expenses on any given fund. If they charge more than that, try finding a different fund that holds similar investments.

A few ETFs to consider:

SPDR S&P 500 Trust (SPY) – holds the largest American companies and gives you exposure to the U.S. stock market

iShares Russell 2000 (IWM) – holds shares in smaller companies that could potentially grow faster than large companies

iShares MSCI EAFE (EFA) – holds shares of large companies based in developed foreign countries

Vanguard Emerging Markets (VWO) – holds shares of companies based in emerging markets like China, India, Brazil and Russia

While holding a broad-based fund like those above will generally give you plenty of exposure to different sectors, Select Sector SPDR Funds are good choices for more exposure to a specific sector.

Adding individual stocks to your portfolio is a matter of choosing 10 or more companies that you think have very strong long-term potential. You should limit your total investment in each to around 2% of your portfolio to limit risk in any particular company.

Since I'll be holding these stocks for decades or more, I like to start with the larger themes before trying to pick individual companies. The idea is to find companies that have very strong forces behind them over the long-term, forces like demographics and economic trends.

Will an aging population need services in any particular sector like healthcare? Will a growing world population and its ever-increasing need for food drive demand in certain agriculture companies? As more of the world goes online, what will that mean for demand of data storage and services?

It is these kinds of forces that will provide a huge tailwind for all the companies in certain sectors and industries. Finding a few of these takes the risk of finding the 'perfect' company.

Once you've narrowed your search down to a few sectors or industries, I like to focus on the very large companies for my individual stock investments. These companies may not grow as quickly as smaller rivals but I'm already taking a risk by investing in a single stock, I want to reduce that risk by investing in companies with the financial power to survive for decades.

I like to get paid for holding an investment in a company so I also look for stocks that pay a dividend. From my list of potential stocks, I weed out those that don't pay a dividend yield of 1% or higher.

Picking from the remaining stocks on your list doesn't have to be complicated. Look over some articles and analysis for each and compare the arguments made. If you've focused on the bigger issues like long-term trends and larger companies, then the future for most of the companies within a theme will look similar.

Investing in Real Estate

There are two ways to invest in real estate, directly and indirectly. Direct investment involves buying residential or commercial property and managing it for the monthly rent return.

Investing indirectly in real estate means buying shares of real estate investment trusts (REITs) or other companies that manage a portfolio of properties.

For a detailed strategy in buying residential or commercial properties for a source of passive income, check out The Passive Income Myth. I outline the process of real estate investing as well as how to earn an income from blogging, stocks and bonds.

We'll focus on indirect real estate investing and REITs in this book. You've got two options when investing in REITs, invest in the individual companies or buy shares of a REIT fund.

Individual REITs invest mostly in commercial property and usually focus on a specific type of property, i.e. storage, office space, warehouses, apartments, industrial and healthcare.

Picking individual REITs is a lot like picking individual stocks, look to the long-term trends and choose a few companies within each trend.

For example, in my own portfolio, I own a couple of REITs that hold industrial properties and a few that own properties in Healthcare. The revolution in U.S. energy production has brought energy costs down in manufacturing and I believe U.S. industrial companies will be able to benefit over the long-term.

The aging U.S. population along with universal healthcare should drive a long-term trend for healthcare companies.

For broad-based exposure to REITs, it's hard to find a better fund than the Vanguard REIT ETF (VNQ). The fund holds over 100 individual REITs and provides instant diversification across all property types and on property spread across the United States.

Investing in Bonds

I detail how to choose bonds for your investing plan in the third book in the series, Step-by-Step Bond Investing. We'll cover the basics here but you should consider getting a more detailed look through the separate book.

Bonds are likely the most overlooked asset class among investors. These investments in the debt issued by companies and governments provide a nearly guaranteed return but most investors neglect the investment altogether.

When you buy a bond, the company promises to pay you an interest payment and to return the price of the bond at the end of a certain number of years. The interest payment usually occurs twice a year and is a fixed amount. Since the regular payments and the final payment are fixed, you immediately know the return on the investment.

As long as the company does not go bankrupt over the life of the bond, you will receive that fixed return. Even in bankruptcy, bond investors get paid before stock investors so you will likely book some kind of return.

Bonds are issued by governments, companies and even by local authorities. Each issuer and individual bond is rated by one of a few credit rating agencies according to riskiness of the company and the investment. It's this rating that helps determine the return that investors will receive.

Bond investing is the one area in which I would not recommend holding exchange traded funds. In a bond fund, the manager is constantly buying and selling individual bonds. This breaks down the guaranteed return that investors receive if they hold a bond until it expires. While bond funds are less risky than stocks or stock funds, you should consider directly investing in bonds for the fixed-income part of your portfolio.

Most of the online investing websites will allow you to buy and hold bond investments. Choose a mix of bonds expiring in different years and from different credit ratings. This will help balance risk and return and provide a constant stream of income into your portfolio.

Yield by Category

AVERAGE YIELD BY CATEGORY   Last Updated: 06/12/2015 05:21 PM

	1Y	2Y	3Y	5Y	7Y	10Y	20Y	30Y+
CDs	.580	1.070	1.530	2.200	2.560	3.190	3.300	---
US Treasuries	.348	.795	1.151	1.768	2.123	2.348	---	2.714
US Treasury Zeroes	---	---	---	---	---	---	---	---
Agencies	.480	.771	1.384	1.953	2.560	2.999	3.747	4.152
AAA Corporates	---	.901	1.266	1.889	---	---	---	4.257
AA Corporates	.454	1.134	1.836	2.372	3.138	3.372	4.225	4.663
A Corporates	.876	1.721	2.201	2.856	3.388	3.879	4.800	5.112
AAA Municipals	.586	1.088	1.483	2.387	2.612	3.245	3.909	4.843
AA Municipals	1.365	2.464	2.412	4.221	4.386	4.714	5.120	5.482
A Municipals	1.328	2.479	3.044	4.238	4.424	4.725	6.167	5.716

Source: E*Trade

Action Steps:

- For investments in stocks and real estate, choose a few ETFs that will give you broad exposure to many investments around a theme.

- For individual investments, start with a larger theme that might play out over decades and boost related stocks.

- Within bonds, diversify your investment across different issuers and time periods.

Step by Step Investing: Maintaining your Portfolio

Once you've set up your investment portfolio, maintaining your investments can be very easy. You will have regular deposits each month coming into your different accounts but do not necessarily need to be investing that money as regularly.

Picking a date every three or six months to invest the cash sitting in your accounts is a better strategy. You'll end up paying less in fees and setting a calendar date helps to keep you from checking in on your investments daily.

Don't worry about missing out on 'hot' investments or a runaway market. Investing is about your long-term strategy and any three- or six-month period isn't going to mean much.

Step 6: Rebalancing your Investments

We've talked briefly about rebalancing but it deserves another look. Rebalancing is just changing your investments around to better match your strategy. Two things might cause you to need to rebalance your investments.

- Your investments in one asset class or within an asset class might have zoomed higher or plunged, making it a different percentage of your total investments. Stocks will outperform bonds over the long-term. Your portfolio that started as 50% in stocks may shift to 60% in stocks as the investments gain in price. Similarly, investments in tech companies may rise more quickly than your investments in utilities companies.

- Your risk tolerance and investing strategy will change over time. Younger investors will have more in stocks but will gradually want to move more to bonds over decades of investing.

The first reason may mean rebalancing every few years while you probably won't need to rebalance on changing risk tolerance more than every ten years.

Taking the time to rebalance means your investments won't stray too far from your plan. If you never rebalanced, your stock investments would be a much larger chunk of your wealth and a stock market crash could seriously derail your ability to meet your financial goals.

With rebalancing, you also avoid getting caught up in investor euphoria around stocks or other assets. Rebalancing helps to sell what has done really well, and might be expensive, while buying investments that might be cheaper.

Two ways to rebalance

Investors typically rebalance their portfolio in one of two ways, annually or by percentage-of-portfolio. Annual rebalancing, or another time-delimited schedule, is done on a set schedule. Percentage-of-portfolio rebalancing sets percentages of the portfolio value for each asset class and sector which the investor wants to keep. The investor rebalances the investments when the percentages vary too much from the targets.

Annual rebalancing is fairly straight-forward. Instead of rebalancing in December, like most investors, try doing it earlier in the year. If you sell your winning investments in December, then capital gains taxes are due almost immediately the next year. If you wait until January, then taxes won't be due until the following year.

If the value of the assets or sectors in your portfolio hasn't changed much from where they started over the year, then it doesn't really make much sense to incur transaction costs or taxes in rebalancing. If the percentage in an asset class or sector is within 5% or 10% of your target, go ahead and just wait another year to rebalance.

The percentage-of-portfolio method requires more management but also makes sense. You are rebalancing because you do not want your portfolio overly exposed to any one asset or group, so it would stand to reason that you would want to rebalance on the percentages within the portfolio. If stocks really take off over a few months then you might want to rebalance regardless of how much time has passed.

The method can be more costly than annual rebalancing depending on how quickly the portfolio percentages change. You won't want to rebalance immediately when an asset class or sector become a larger part of your portfolio. Wait until the percentages move further from your plan. If you planned on having 40% of your wealth in stocks, you might wait until it is 50% to sell some stocks to rebalance into bonds.

A combination of the two methods can provide the best of both worlds. You'll be investing new money every six months anyway so use your new investment to rebalance your portfolio by buying more of some investments and less of others. The idea of rebalancing isn't about timing the markets but about keeping as close to your plan as possible without paying too much in fees.

How to Know when it's time to sell

The easiest answer to when you should sell an investment is…never. Your decision to buy an investment should be based on long-term factors that span decades, not near-term analysis. Holding an investment for several decades will cut down on trading fees, taxes and reduce the risk of bad investment decisions.

Your investments in ETFs do not generally need to be sold because they are broad-based across many companies. Unless something catastrophic occurs to change the future of the entire sector or industry, you shouldn't need to sell a fund unless your risk tolerance changes.

There are a few reasons why you would sell some or all of your investment.

- If it becomes public that management has been acting unethically or lying to investors. Similarly, if the company has expanded into a line of business that dramatically changes it from the reason for which you invested. These do not generally occur often.

- You may want to sell some of your investments for normal rebalancing every few years. Selling an investment will mean trading fees so you might just consider shifting your regular investment purchases into other investments instead. It may happen though, that one stock or investment soars and you need to reduce your exposure. I would not let any one company account for more than 5% or 6% of my total portfolio.

- You may need to sell some investments when you do your asset rebalancing as well. This is the very long-term rebalancing you do maybe every ten years to adjust your risk across stocks, bonds and real estate.

Action Steps:

- Determine how often you will rebalance your investments and whether you will do it when percentages shift from your targets or by calendar date

- Commit to only checking your portfolio value at set intervals. This will help reduce the temptation to make quick buy or sell decisions.

A Special Request

I hope you've enjoyed Step-by-Step Investing and found the advice to be helpful in putting together your investing strategy. Throughout the book, I've tried to emphasize the benefit to a simple and basic strategy that meets YOUR financial goals. There's no lack of ways to complicate your investing strategy but the simplest approach will get you to where you want to be with the least amount of headache and sleepless nights.

I'd like to ask one favor as you finish reading the book. Reader reviews are extremely important to the success of a book on Amazon. Reviews play a big part in determining the rank of a book and how many people see it when searching.

If you found the book to be helpful, would you please leave a review on the Amazon page?

It's really easy to do and does not have to be a long, detailed review.

Please click here to leave a review on Amazon

- Just go to the book's page on Amazon (or through the link above) and click on "customer reviews" or scroll down and click on "Write a customer review"

- Your review can be as short as a sentence or as long as you like. Just try describing what you liked about the book and any particular points from a chapter.

I always appreciate honest reviews. Thank you so much!

Resources

Round out your investing plan with the best investments in dividends, emerging markets and bonds. Check out the other three books in the Step-by-Step series:

Learn how to put dividend stocks in your portfolio and money in your pocket! This book covers income investments like REITs, MLPs and dividend stocks that have provided strong returns and a regular cash return. ***Click here to buy Step-by-Step Dividend Investing.***

Learn the secret to bond investing and how to balance your investments with safety. This book covers how to buy bonds and a simple strategy that will provide a stable income stream you can live on. ***Click here to buy Step-by-Step Bond Investing.***

Learn how to add growth to your investments through stocks from the fastest growing countries in the world. This book shows you how to boost returns and lower risk by diversifying in emerging markets. ***Click here to buy Step-by-Step Emerging Market Investing.***

See through the BS and scams in passive income strategies to start building a real source of income today in blogging, real estate, stocks and bonds.

NO fluff, NO theories, and NO sugar coating – just the detailed process on how I put together an income from four sources and make money whether I work or not. ***Click here to buy The Passive Income Myth.***

News and Professional Organizations

Check out these websites for news and detailed data on investments covered in this book.

Bloomberg – Business and finance news resource that keeps it objective. You'll see some analyst commentary but the ideas are usually fairly balanced.

Morningstar – Professional source of data and company financial information. There is a lot of analysis and advice on the site. Most of it is objective and helpful but avoid using it to make short-term investment decisions.

National Association of Real Estate Investment Trusts (NAREIT) – Information, news and research on REITs and Real Estate

Yahoo Finance – An excellent resource for stock information including charts, data and headlines.

Investing and Personal Finance Blogs

Check out these blogs for more advice on personal finance and meeting your long-term goals. Blogs here were chosen for their rational and measured perspective, favoring a long-term approach instead of get-rich-quick schemes.

PeerFinance101 – My blog on personal finance and achieving financial freedom. Financial freedom isn't about getting rich but getting the life you want and making money decisions around that goal. Share your own stories of financial success or learn from others stories.

Side Hustle Nation–A community of part-time entrepreneurs earning financial independence through small business. It's a great resource for finding your passion and turning your hobby into a money-maker.

Barbara Friedberg Personal Finance–Barbara worked as an investment portfolio manager before launching her blog, offering advice following many of the tenets in this book. It's a great site focused on investing and building wealth.

Club Thrifty – Holly and Greg were able to ditch their 9-to-5 jobs after learning to manage their money. The blog focuses on ways to spend smartly, cut debt and earn extra income.

Bible Money Matters – Peter hits all the topics in personal finance but he also talks about faith and family. It's a great blog that will help you lead an inspired life.

Made in the USA
San Bernardino, CA
22 April 2018